PHOTOGRAPHY BY DAVID UTTLEY

Thirst

Water is life. This truth has never been more poignant than in rural Africa. Clean water lies at the core of many challenges facing the African people. Caught in a horrible cycle of sickness and disease, contaminated water destroys the strength and development of African families and communities. This leads to extreme poverty, lack of education, and greater illnesses.

In sub-Saharan Africa alone, millions of people lack access to the basic necessity of clean drinking water. Diarrheal disease due to easily preventable causes claims the lives of thousands of young children. Contaminated drinking water also accelerates the African AIDS pandemic. Waterborne bacteria, normally mild for healthy individuals, becomes an incurable death sentence for those with a weakened immune system.

Trapped in this downward spiral, it becomes difficult, if not impossible, for these African people to break out of their terrible plight.

Musician and activist Bono accepted the 2005 TED Prize with a passionate talk arguing that, *"Africa is bursting into flames while we all stand around with watering cans."*

Through The Thirst Project, we are building wells in communities where there is no access to clean water. This book of images is dedicated to that effort. We each can do our part to meet this overwhelming need.

As the deer pants
for streams of water.

so my soul pants for you, O God.

My soul thirsts for God, for the living God.
When can I go and meet with God?

My tears have been my food day and night, while men say to me all day long, "Where is your God?"

REAL.
(MAN.REN'04)
DALL
WE CHARGE PHONE

These things I remember as I pour out my soul:
how I used to go with the multitude, leading the procession to
the house of God, with shouts of joy and
thanksgiving among the festive throng.

Why are you downcast, O my soul?
Why so disturbed within me?
Put your hope in God, for I will yet praise him,
my Savior and my God.

My soul is downcast within me;
therefore I will remember you
from the land of the Jordan,
the heights of Hermon—from Mount Mizar.

Deep calls to deep in the roar of your waterfalls;
all your waves and breakers
have swept over me.

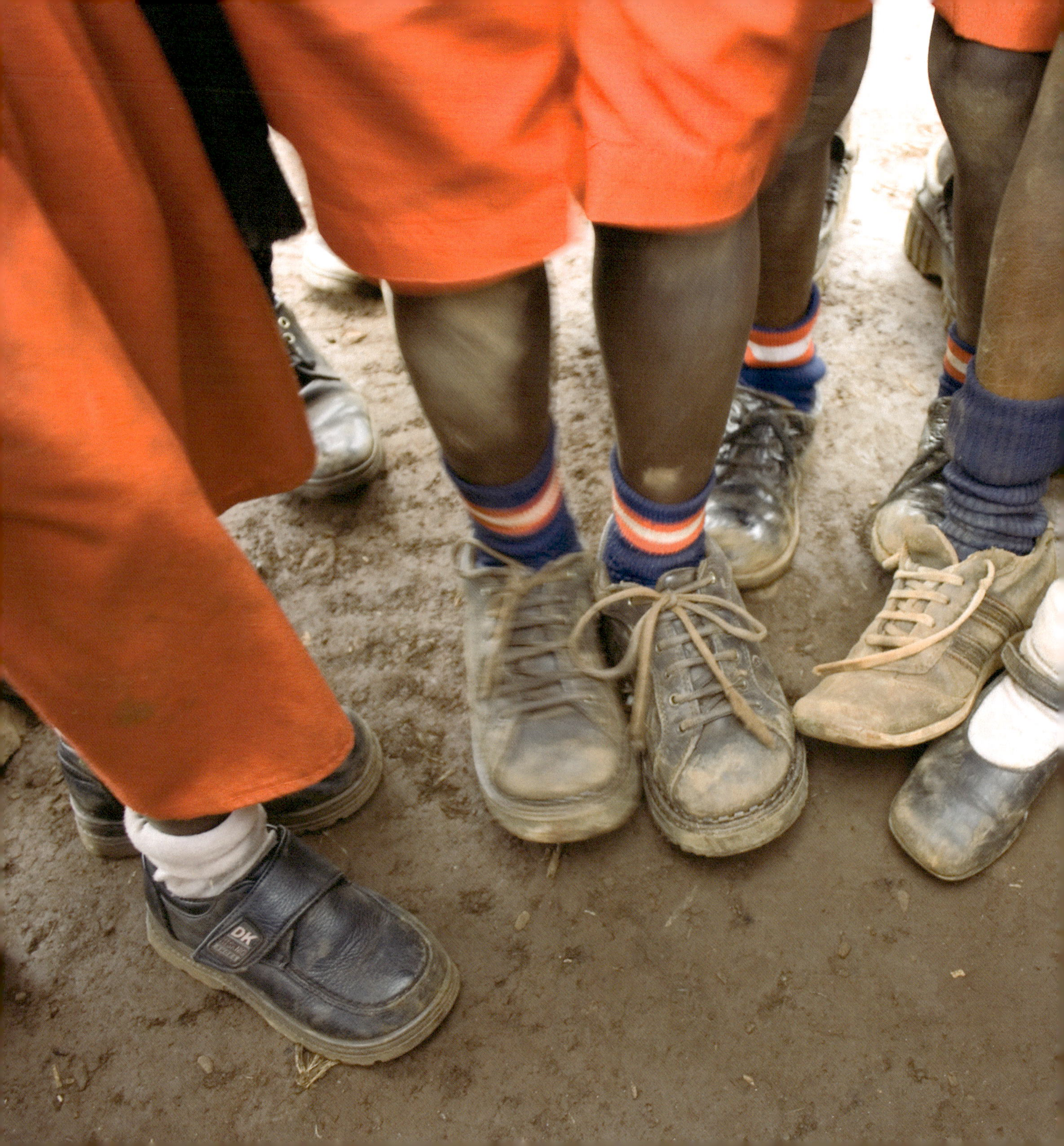

By day the Lord directs his love,
at night his song is with me—
a prayer to the God of my life.

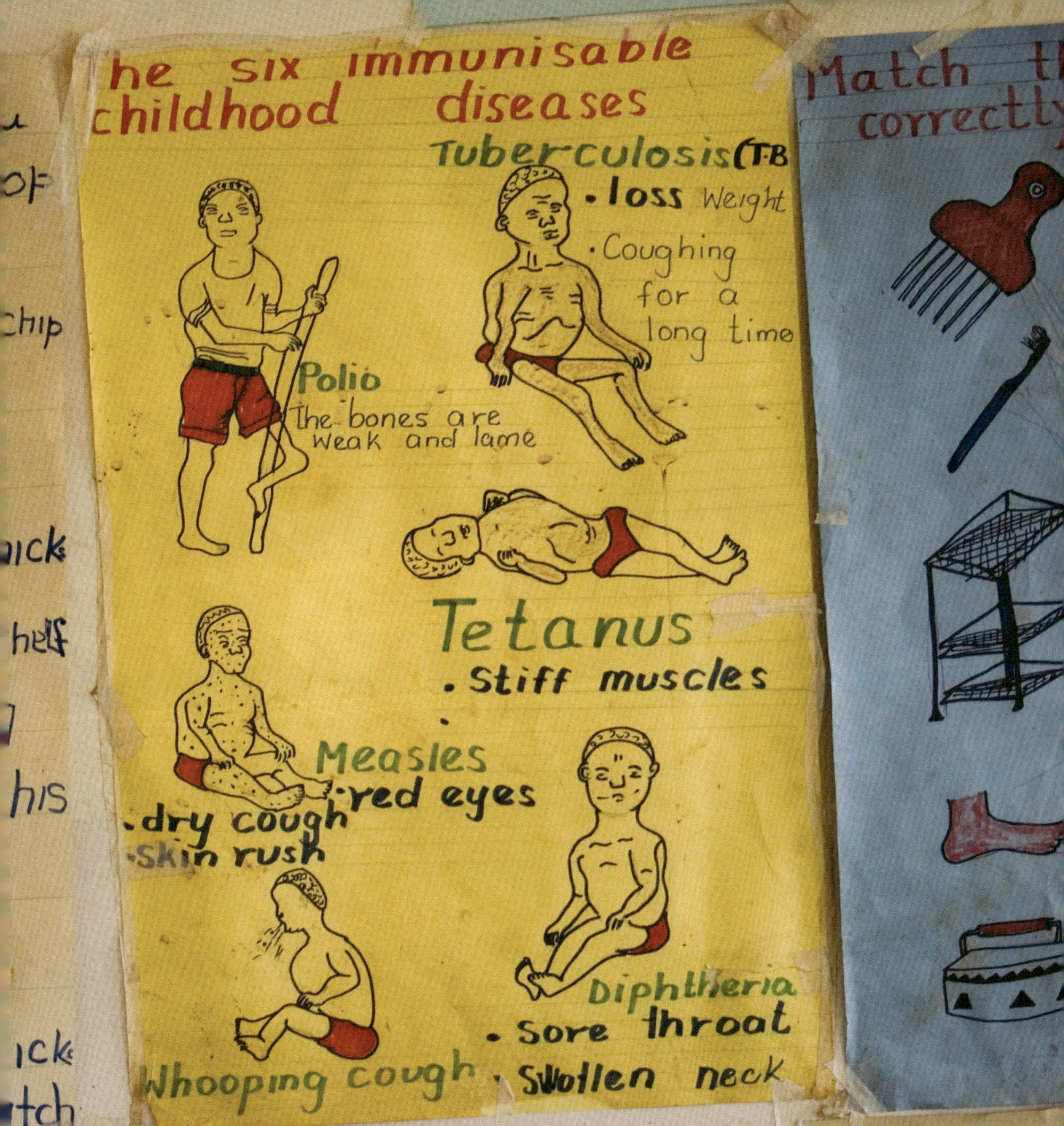
The six immunisable childhood diseases
Tuberculosis (T.B)
. loss weight
. Coughing for a long time
Polio
The bones are weak and lame
Tetanus
. stiff muscles
.
Measles
. red eyes
. dry cough
. skin rush
Whooping cough
Diphtheria
. sore throat
. swollen neck
Match the correctly

I say to God my Rock,
"Why have you forgotten me?
Why must I go about mourning,
oppressed by the enemy?"

My bones suffer mortal agony
as my foes taunt me, saying to me all day long,
"Where is your God?"

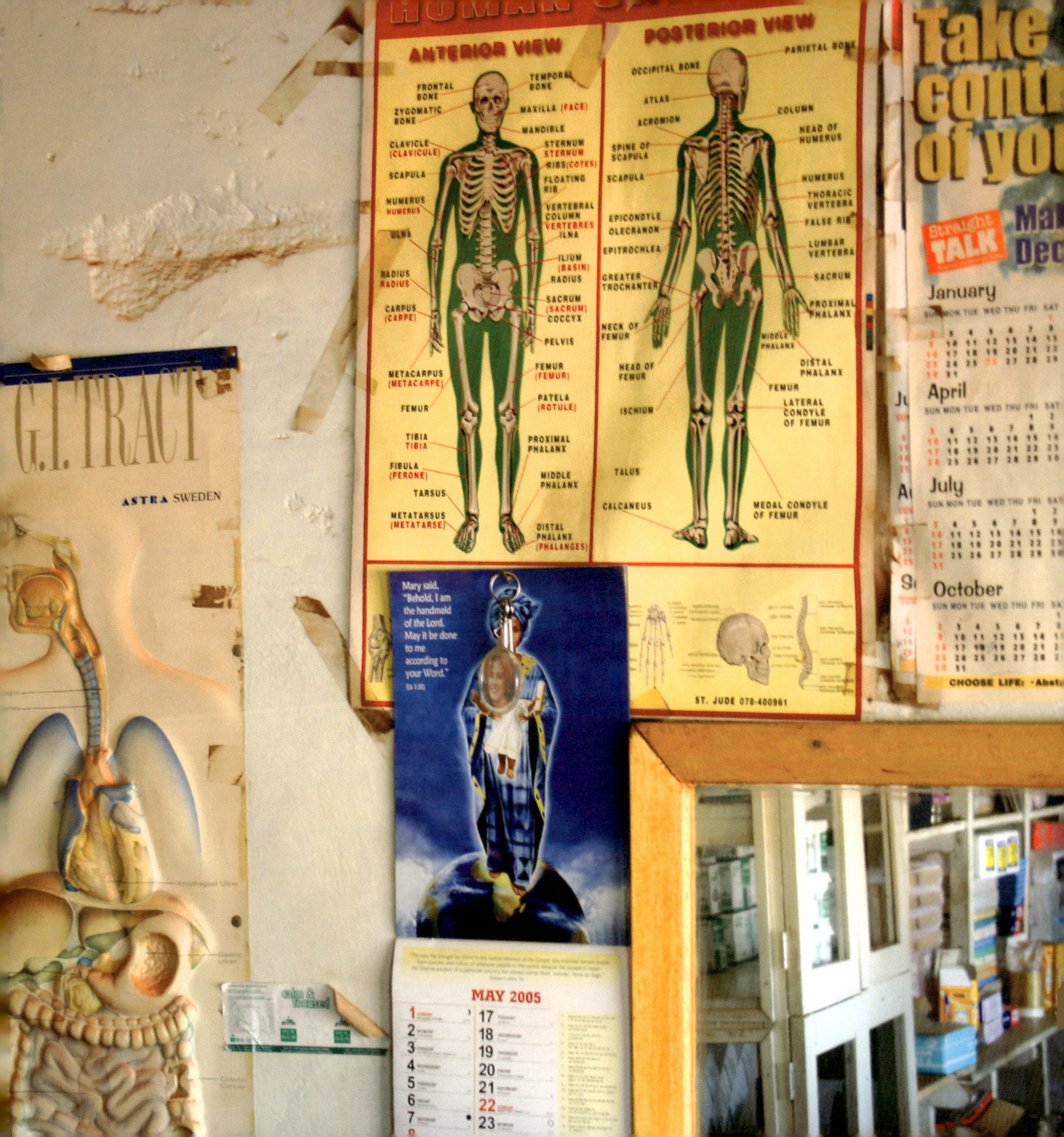
HUMAN SKELETON
ANTERIOR VIEW
POSTERIOR VIEW
FRONTAL BONE
TEMPORAL BONE
ZYGOMATIC BONE
MAXILLA (FACE)
MANDIBLE
CLAVICLE (CLAVICULE)
STERNUM STERNUM
RIBS (COTES)
SCAPULA
FLOATING RIB
HUMERUS HUMERUS
VERTEBRAL COLUMN VERTEBRES ILNA
ULNA
ILIUM (BASIN)
RADIUS RADIUS
RADIUS
CARPUS (CARPE)
SACRUM (SACRUM)
COCCYX
PELVIS
METACARPUS (METACARPE)
FEMUR (FEMUR)
FEMUR
PATELA (ROTULE)
TIBIA TIBIA
PROXIMAL PHALANX
FIBULA (PERONE)
MIDDLE PHALANX
TARSUS
METATARSUS (METATARSE)
DISTAL PHALANX (PHALANGES)
OCCIPITAL BONE
PARIETAL BONE
ATLAS
COLUMN
ACROMION
HEAD OF HUMERUS
SPINE OF SCAPULA
SCAPULA
HUMERUS
THORACIC VERTEBRA
EPICONDYLE
OLECRANON
FALSE RIB
EPITROCHLEA
LUMBAR VERTEBRA
GREATER TROCHANTER
SACRUM
NECK OF FEMUR
PROXIMAL PHALANX
MIDDLE PHALANX
HEAD OF FEMUR
DISTAL PHALANX
ISCHIUM
FEMUR
LATERAL CONDYLE OF FEMUR
TALUS
CALCANEUS
MEDAL CONDYLE OF FEMUR
ST. JUDE 078-400961
G.I. TRACT
ASTRA SWEDEN
Mary said,
"Behold, I am the handmaid of the Lord. May it be done to me according to your Word."
(Lk 1:38)
MAY 2005
1 17
2 18
3 19
4 20
5 21
6 22
7 23
Take contr of you
Straight TALK
Ma Dec
January
SUN MON TUE WED THU FRI SAT
April
SUN MON TUE WED THU FRI SAT
July
SUN MON TUE WED THU FRI SAT
October
SUN MON TUE WED THU FRI SAT
CHOOSE LIFE · Abst

Why are you downcast, O my soul?

Why so disturbed within me?

OBEY
YOUR
THIRST

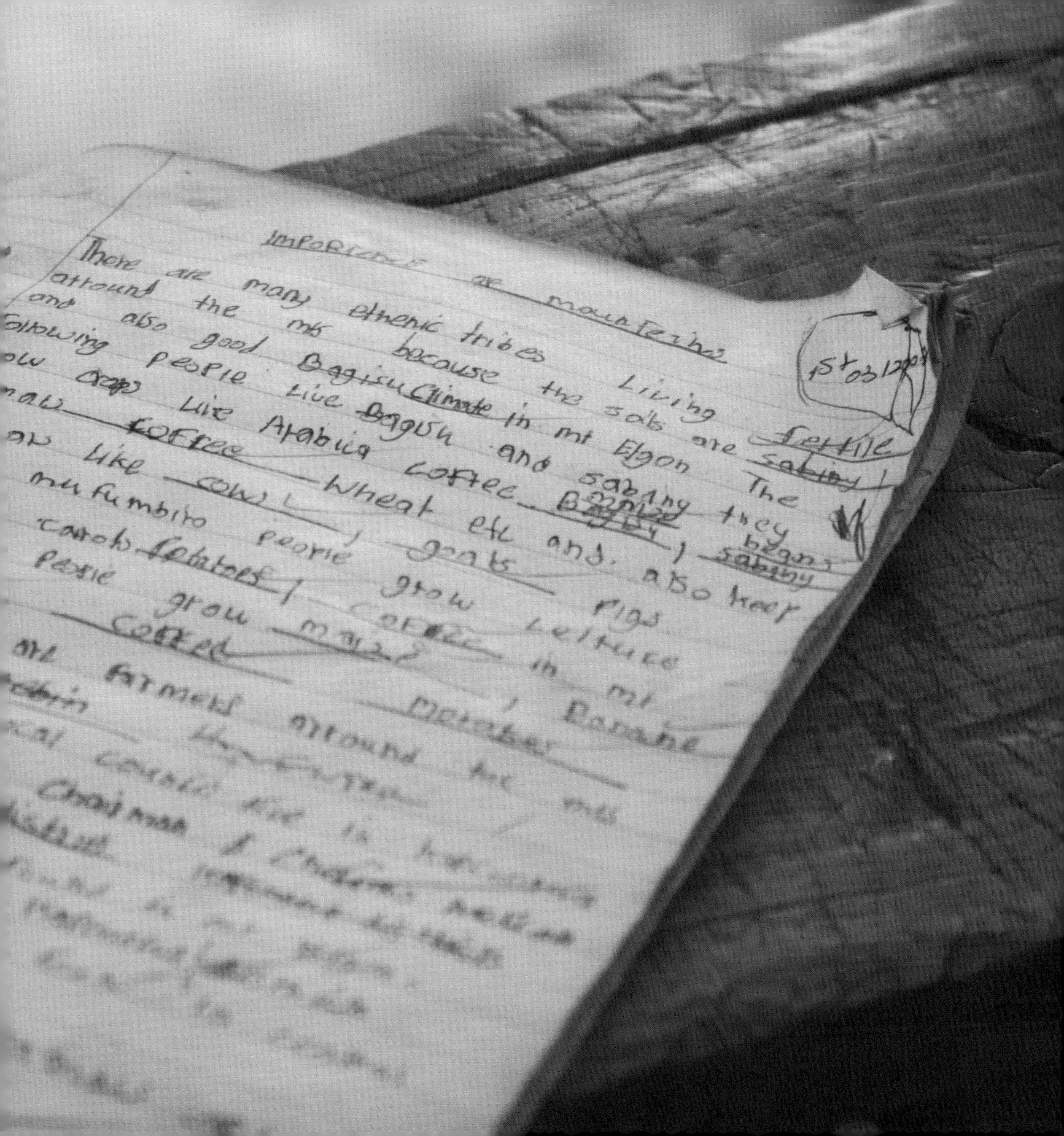

<u>IMPORTANCE OF MOUNTAINS</u>

There are many ethnic tribes living around the mts because the soils are <u>fertile</u> and also good. Bagisu <u>Climate</u> in mt Elgon and sabiny they

following people live Bagisu like Arabica coffee, beans sabiny

like <u>cow</u> wheat etc and. also keep <u>sabiny</u>

mufumbiro people goats pigs grow lettuce

carrots <u>potatoes</u> grow maize coffee in mt

<u>coffee</u> Banana

are farmers around the mts

local council

Chairman & Chairman

district

Put your hope in God, for I will yet praise him,
my Savior and my God.

GUVU 32

MTN 200
CELTEL 400
MGO 400
UTL 200
INT 1200

Help the people of Africa by donating generously to The Thirst Project.
Your gift will have an incredible impact in people's lives and help end this cycle of despair.

Please consider giving an online donation through Blood:Water Mission
www.bloodwatermission.org (mention The Thirst Project)
BLOOD:WATER MISSION is a grassroots organization that empowers communities
to work against the HIV/AIDS and water crises in Africa.

For more information:
The Thirst Project, P.O. Box 1523
Sisters, OR 97759

info@thethirstproject.org
www.thethirstproject.org

Thirst
©2008 The DesignWorks Group
www.thedesignworksgroup.com
Photography ©2007 by David Uttley
Scripture text: Psalm 42, NIV
ISBN: 0979316413
ISBN 13: 9780979316418

Printed in the United States
129938LV00002B